52 Secrets
Success, Fun & Fulfillment

I *Almost* Missed My Life
Don't *Miss* Yours

Remember to always
"Enjoy the Ride!"

Debra

For information address:
E Ticket Enterprises, Inc.
P.O. Box 23127
Santa Barbara, CA 93121
877-400-0007

Author's email: Debra@DebraRussell.com

www.DebraRussell.com

ISBN 0-9720444-0-X

Printed in the United States of America.

Praise For Debra's Book Russell's

I *Almost* Missed My Life

Heartland Reviews - Bob Spear, Chief Reviewer
"*I Almost Missed My Life* is an excellent motivational
book. The advice the author gives is not just the usual
rah rah pap of the genre, but is practical and do-able.
We gave it a four heart rating." ♥♥♥♥

"Debra Russell brings the charm and wit of her tumul-
tuous life into easy lessons for us all. The format is
excellent for a path to understanding yourself and
getting the most out of your life. And you can't help
falling in love with the author who shares and guides
with such love and openness." —*Ellen May*

"I have read many self help books but this one ranks as
one of my favorites. It is easy and enjoyable to read
and is packed full of powerful techniques you can use
immediately to improve your life. Read the book and
start enjoying the ride." —*Bruce W. Chelmsford, MA.*

"This is the first book in years that took me only one
day to read completely - I didn't put it down."
—*Amada Pichardo*

"Don't read this book unless you are ready to give up
the games, because once you learn these easy lessons
you won't have any more excuses." —*Corabel Shofner*

"It is so easy!!! It is a short, easy to follow book...it
would be a shame to miss it and miss out on the rest
of your life!" —*Belmont Trapp*

I dedicate this book to my children, Leland and Kashina. You are the light of my life and I love you more than words can express. I am forever grateful for the gift of being your mother. I also dedicate this book to your children and theirs and on and on...Thank you for being my family!

Acknowledgments

I would like to thank the following people for their part in the creation of this book. My children for the lessons I've learned from them, the love they've brought to my life and for always believing in me. Mimi Peak for her unending friendship and support. David Chiu for being a great friend and being a genuine model of possibility thinking. All of the teachers, mentors and role models whose work I have been inspired by and learned from including: Anthony Robbins, Dr. Wayne Dyer, Dr. Norman Vincent Peale, the Dalai Lama and many more...and finally, Edward Clapp and Linda Farrell for their thoughtful editing support.

Contents

52 Secrets To More Success, Fun & Fulfillment

I *Almost* Missed My Life
Don't Miss Yours

Introduction

I *Almost* Missed My Life

Have you ever been at a critical decision point in your life but you felt frozen? Do you know the feeling of "damned if you do, damned if you don't?" That's where I was in 1985 at age thirty-two. Fortunately, our lives can change in an instant and mine did that day when I decided to create the life I really wanted — *not the one I was living!*

A Brief Account...

On the next few pages you'll find a quick snapshot of my life. I hope it will give you insight into the circumstances that led me to an important moment of decision that changed my life forever. I have given you the highlights, rather than all the graphic details, because they simply aren't important now. Rather than dwelling on yesterday, I focus my attention on living each day to the fullest and anticipating tomorrow with great enthusiasm!

Every person's story is important, especially to that person. We've all been through negative experiences that we can easily hold on to — experiences that can drag us down. Whether someone is dealing with a boss they don't like or whether a person has had a much more traumatic life than I did, each story matters.

Once I met a very successful woman who at the tender age of twenty-one had given birth to seven (that's right — seven) children. She was the daughter of a crop picker and had even tried to commit suicide on three separate occasions. When I met her, I said, "My God, I thought I'd had a rough childhood!" She replied in an almost angelic voice, "Oh honey, it's not about that. You see, God just keeps sending you lessons until you get it and I was just one tough bitch." I burst into laughter at the sincerity with which she sweetly delivered those words.

Whatever you are dealing with, you can breakthrough it. There is a way to get past, through, around, under or over any barrier. There is a way to utilize your past or even your current situation to create a future filled with more fun, love, success, excitement and fulfillment. *It's never too late to create the life you really want!*

A Rich and Colorful History

I grew up in Mississippi with my mom, dad and older brother. During the day I went to school, played with friends, took dance lessons and generally acted like a kid.

The challenge was during the nights. From my earliest memories, my father came into my room at night and "touched me" inappropriately. I enjoyed my daytime life, which was filled with activities and friends; I suffered through my nighttime life, which was scary and surreal. In spite of my prayers asking Jesus to keep my father away, his nighttime visits continued.

One *morning* my father approached me and out of the horror of his invading my *daytime* life, I stood up for myself and made him stop.

When I was sixteen, the summer after tenth grade, my parents divorced — quite a relief to me — and my mother and I moved to California. When I got there, I hated it! It was the late 60s and sex, drugs and rock n' roll scared me. Also, I missed my boyfriend and his family — especially his mother — and I longed to be back in their arms in Mississippi.

When my boyfriend's little brother, who suffered from muscular dystrophy, died that first summer, I went home to Mississippi for the funeral. I did not want to go back to California and I had a brilliant solution — get married. At age sixteen, I married my boyfriend. My childhood friend, Corabel, still likes to recall, with amusement, that she had to come home from summer camp for my wedding. I attended eleventh grade in Greenwood, Mississippi as a married "woman" and ditched twelfth grade.

One month after my eighteenth birthday, I gave birth to my precious son in an Army hospital in Aberdeen, Maryland. I was frightened out of my wits but the trauma of giving birth passed quickly when I experienced being a mom. I was much too young but I was totally devoted to my son.

The marriage was a different story. We tried, but our relationship was a typical teenage romance fraught with all the drama and pain of adolescence. Inevitably, I ran away from that marriage and, at age nineteen, I arrived in California with my eighteen-month-old son on my hip. California — ironic don't you think?

I got a job and met a woman in my office who set me up with her son. I thought he was wonderful — not at all like the "hicks" in Mississippi. He was a poet and writer and was very loving and attentive toward my son and me. He wanted to get married; I didn't want to be alone. So the wedding was on. That was only six weeks after we met — I was good at making seemingly inspired decisions.

One of the first times I was aware of my inner voice, my *knowing,* was the night before I married him. I told my mother I had a bad feeling about this and that I didn't think I should marry him. Her response was to pull out 10 mg of Valium to calm my pre-wedding jitters and the next day I was married — again.

I loved my new husband and I trusted him completely and totally. After four months of marriage, I saw a report proving that everything he had ever told me about his life was a lie. My new husband was a clinically diagnosed, pathological liar. I was devastated and came very close to committing suicide.

4

Fortunately, I managed to stop myself just in time. The only thing between death and me was the love I had for my two-year-old son and my unborn daughter (I was three months pregnant).

I felt betrayed and trapped. The next two years were crammed with my husband's lies and my own self-doubt. Finally he left town for a few days and I had just enough time for the fog to lift. I thought seriously about the consequences a life with him would have on my children and I knew I couldn't stay.

It took the last ounce of strength I had left to leave him. Even though I did it, I was sad, frightened and felt incapable of ever loving or trusting another man. Besides, I was positive that no one would ever love me or want me again anyway. I was twenty-two and had been married and divorced twice with two children from two different fathers — get real.

Now what? I had the responsibility of raising my two children alone and I needed a skill that would help me earn a decent living. Since I had no financial resources, I spent almost a year on welfare while I attended barber college. I hated being on welfare. It was embarrassing that I had ended up in that situation, but it seemed necessary at the time. During my time in barber college, I had to deal with the consequences of my decision to divorce my second husband. He took me to court to try to take my children away; he called constantly and even stalked me. He did everything he could to plague my life.

But I made it through. In part because of someone I'd known since I was thirteen who had always had a crush on me and who I treasured as a friend. Dennis gave me emotional support through barber college and the aftermath of my divorce. A year later he asked me to marry him.

At twenty-three, I felt used up, tired, and frightened. While I wasn't in love with Dennis, he was safe and I cared for him so I married my *friend*. During the ten years we were together, I had the space and security I needed to heal.

So there I was.

At thirty-one, I was beginning to feel tugs at the edge of my consciousness that I could have a better life. I think that in my heart of hearts I knew that I needed to leave my marriage but, I was afraid to face the consequences. How could I put my children through that again? How could I hurt Dennis when he had been so supportive? How could I live with the social stigma of three failed marriages? Besides, every major choice I had made up until that point was like jumping out of the frying pan into the fire.

I decided to go to a therapist. Some part of me was probably trying to avoid making a decision but the main reason I went was this: I had made every major decision in my life out of a need to avoid some painful situation. I felt that *it was time for me to make an intelligent, thoughtful choice about my life*. After a year, the therapist told me that there was nothing else she could do for me — I simply needed to decide.

I came home that day feeling completely dejected and alone, but knowing she was right. I had to make a decision. Suddenly, I got an inspiration. I've noticed over the years that I often become inspired when something becomes a *must* rather than a *should*. That time was no exception. It was clear that I needed a new perspective and that's when I came up with the *Rocking Chair Test*.

The Rocking Chair Test

I imagined I was ninety-six, generally healthy, but at the end of my life. I sat in an old rocking chair, closed my eyes and pretended to age myself. I felt my body get weaker, slumping in the chair. I imagined that I would be passing on in a few hours but I had no fear. I knew it was my time and this was simply my opportunity to reflect.

I asked myself, "What do I want to be feeling at this very moment?" And all of a sudden the following answer popped out of my mouth, "I want to say, now that was an *E Ticket Ride!*" It had been years since Disneyland had used those ticket books but I remembered the elation I had felt at the end of my favorite rides. Sure, you could use the A, B, C, or D tickets. But it was the *E Tickets* that got you on the best rides in the park. The thrill of imagining that I could have that elation about my life was overwhelming. My body was filled with positive energy and I knew — *that* would be a life worth living!

It was difficult to bring myself back to my *Rocking Chair Test* but I managed to return to that state and I asked the question again, "What else do I want to be feeling at this very moment?" The answer was almost as intense but produced a different emotion. This time the answer was, "I know what I don't want to be feeling; I don't want to be feeling any regrets. I don't want to be asking myself, 'What if I had...' Or saying, 'Maybe I should have... I could have... If only I had...' "

With these two newfound guiding principles — *E Ticket Ride* and *No Regrets*, I played out the current situation and the answer became clear immediately. If I was going to be married, it had to be with someone I loved as a *husband* and I knew I could never have that with my *friend*. I wanted more. It was time for me to proactively create the life I wanted but it was going to take courage and commitment. I still had to deal with the consequences that decision would bring (hurting people I loved, the stigma of being divorced three times, tight finances, on and on). I had to deal with those consequences *while* beginning to create my new life. Easy? No! Necessary? Yes!

How do you want to feel when looking back on your life? What would make you happy and fulfilled? *The Rocking Chair Test* is a great way to gain perspective about the choices you are making today and where those choices will lead you to tomorrow. The future is inevitable but what it looks like is yours to create!

At any moment you can *decide to create* the life you *really* want. That life is waiting for you, all you have to do is claim it. I did! But I almost missed the wonderful life I have now. I've raised two healthy, independent and loving children. I have a career traveling the world helping people, I go skydiving, take comedy classes, write books, audition for plays, and enjoy wonderful friends. I gave up my dancing at age sixteen but, at age forty-four, I took up Argentine Tango. Now I make exciting sojourns to Buenos Aires, teach when I can and every so often I strut my stuff on stage.

That's the life of my dreams, my *E Ticket Ride*, the life I *almost* missed. What's yours? What do you want to do, be, have and create in your life?

52 Secrets

On the following pages you'll find 52 secrets — a year's worth of opportunities should you choose to use them weekly — to create a life filled with love, success, fun, fulfillment and more. Each secret is something that I have personally used that has helped me experience my life more fully. These secrets have helped me increased my financial success, given me greater confidence, allowed me to make more of a positive difference in the lives of others, and have helped me be a better role model for my children.

One important thread that you'll find running through-out this book is this: **All the secrets are within *your* power**. Each one is related to directing your own perceptions, thinking, behaviors and actions. Many, if not most, people let what happens in the external world determine their happiness, their success, and the love, fun, excitement and passion they experience. The secrets in this book are all based on taking charge of your own experience, of this won-derful adventure called — life.

Ultimately, the fun, excitement, passion, love, suc-cess and fulfillment you'll have will come from within you.

Get The Most From This Book

Use what you learn! The more actively you engage in applying the secrets in this book, the more impact they will have. I encourage you to start and keep a journal because writing things down has been proven to increase success in learning and reaching goals. The *Give It A Go* assignments are designed to get you started but, be creative. There are unlimited applications for these powerful secrets so make sure you experiment and have fun using what you are learning in all aspects of your life and work!

Surround Yourself With Positive Energy. The environ-ment you are in, the people you spend your time with will have an impact on helping (or hindering) your ability to create a life you love living. Make sure you seek out a network of people who encourage, support and challenge you.

Be consistent. The more regularly you read and apply the secrets, the more impact they will have in your life.

Have Fun With It! Experiment and play wit the secrets. Share what you are learning. Make it a game!

10

Introduction

Life is there to be lived fully. Jump in with both feet; splash around; have some fun; go for your dreams and always remember to...enjoy the ride!
—*Debra Russell*

www.DebraRussell.com

1

Begin With The End In Mind

To create the life you desire you must begin by deciding what you truly want. So often we don't think we have a choice; it is easy to look at our circumstances and feel like victims. Stop now. Clear your mind of what you think you can and/or cannot do. Clear your mind of what you think is or is not possible. Once you have done that, then you are free to imagine and *choose* your future.

The truth is that you've already begun the process. Since you are reading this book, your unconscious mind — your inner voice/guidance (and maybe your conscious also) is leading you to change something. What is it? If you were free to create any life (which you are), what would you want to do or create, what kind of person would you want to be, and what things would you like to have?

I spent too many years deciding what I wanted for the future based on my past. For example, I did not graduate from high school so becoming general manager of a multi-million dollar company (which I did) was not even something I could imagine back then. I spent my time building my future based upon the shaky ground of my past experiences and upon whatever current problems I found myself facing.

The key is to keep your eyes focused on the future you *really* want. The past is only valuable when you use it as a stepping-stone to create a successful tomorrow. Clearly defining what you want (in any situation) and then working backwards from that is the most important tool in getting anything and everything you desire.

Give It A Go

Begin a journal. Start by brainstorming everything you would like to be, do, have and create in your life. Take the *Rocking Chair Test* for inspiration. The end I have in mind is to always feel that my life is/was an *E Ticket Ride* and that I have *no regrets*. What do you *really* want? Make sure you write it down!

———————◆———————

Live out your imagination, not your history.
—*Stephen Covey*

———————◆———————

2

Decide and Commit

It has been said that the act of making a decision is power. Once you have clearly defined what you want, you must then *decide* that you will create it. Decision and commitment will be the impetus to get you going and also the fuel to keep you going until you reach your goals and dreams.

Indecision is a common malady in our world and it creates a drain of precious life energy. Have you ever noticed how much time and energy you can invest in *trying* to decide something? Most people find that they feel much better and have greater energy *after* they make a decision.

Fear and lack of belief in myself used to keep me from making real decisions about the life I wanted. But my biggest decision-making barrier was this: I always wanted to know *how* I would accomplish something before I would decide to go for it. The people that I know who are very successful in creating whatever they want, tend to *decide first* and figure out *how* later.

There is a wonderful quote by Goethe that I have referred to many times and that I whole-heartedly believe.

> Until one is committed, there is hesitancy, the chance to draw back, always ineffectiveness. Concerning all acts of initiative (and creation), there is one elementary truth, the ignorance of which kills countless ideas and splendid plans: that the moment one definitely commits oneself, then providence moves too.
>
> All sorts of things occur to help one that would never otherwise have occurred. A whole stream of events issues from the decision, raising in one's favor all manner of unforeseen incidents and meetings and material assistance, which no man could have dreamed would have come his way.
>
> Whatever you can do, or dream you can, begin it. Boldness has genius, power and magic in it. Begin it now.

Give It A Go
Write down what you want for yourself and why you are totally committed to creating that in your life. If you were to go for these goals 100%, what are all of the benefits you can think of? What are the potential consequences if you don't give it your all? Strengthen your emotional resolve.

16

Always bear in mind that your own resolution
to success is more important than any other
one thing. —*Abraham Lincoln*

3

Practice Outcome Thinking

Learning that I could direct my own thinking was one of my greatest breakthroughs, in being able to create my *E Ticket Life*. I used to accept that I was stuck with whatever I thought and believed and that there was nothing I could do about that. Worse yet, I believed that whatever I thought, was actually the truth and in a way, it was. My lack of belief in myself caused me to feel and act in ways that almost insured failure. The question is — how do you direct your thinking?

First — You must stay focused on what you want (not what you don't want). This applies in any situation. When you're not getting what you want, stop and ask yourself this question: "What do I really want?" or "What is my outcome here?" Just clarifying this will help you to move you forward.

Second — Choose thinking that supports your outcome. Ask yourself this: "How would I need to think or what would I need to believe in order to accomplish this outcome?" For example: When I was first thinking of giving seminars, I told a friend. His first response was, "You could never do that. You're too shy and reserved. Besides, you don't have any experience." I was hurt and afraid that he was right. Fortunately, by then I had learned that I had a choice in what to think.

One choice I had was to accept his view, accept *his* thinking. But if I did, I knew that I would never follow my dream. My other option was to choose to think or believe something that would support my outcome. I thought about it for days and finally decided on the following thinking or perspective: "I was painfully shy when I first became a hairstylist, but I learned how to communicate well with individuals. I can learn this too. Besides, he doesn't know what's in my heart and this is something I *really* want. I'll show him! I not only can do this, I am committed to it." I consciously chose thinking that would help me realize my goal.

Give It A Go

Write down at least three of your goals. Then write down the thinking/beliefs that you need to help you reach those goals. You may not feel certain about this new thinking right away. That's ok. The certainty will come with practice, time and new results.

You are today where your thoughts have brought you; you will be tomorrow where your thoughts take you. —*James Lane Allen*

4

Act As If

How do you go from the new thinking, the new beliefs that you've chosen to actually having certainty that they are true? It's much easier than you may think. You *act as if* you believe them until you do.

Even though my career takes me all over the world speaking and training, I used to have an intense phobia about public speaking. After I was forced to take a class in college, Public Speaking 101, I decided that I was going to get over my fear. I joined a great public speaking club called Toastmasters International. Although, I went every Monday morning at 6:30 a.m. for an entire year, I never conquered my fear.

The reason was because I had a mantra, "I'm so scared. I hate this. I'm no good at it." I repeated these phrases constantly and of course, I continued to feel that way. Then I went to a seminar with Anthony Robbins and he taught the "Act As If" principle. I thought, well, it can't hurt so, I'll try it with my public speaking. Several times a day I began to say things to myself like, "I love public speaking. It's so much fun to be on stage. Every time I do a speech, I get better and better. I really love it!" Next, I pretended that I believed it. I talked like I believed it, I walked like I believed it, I visualized confidently speaking to thousands of people and I redirected my thinking every time I fell back into the old mantra. After a very short period of time, maybe one or two weeks, I was looking forward to speaking.

In many interviews I've heard with actors, singers and other performers, they have told stories of how they would stand in front of a mirror and pretend they were acting in a play or receiving an academy award. Jim Carey once said that in his early days when he felt scared or uncertain about his career, he would drive up to a hill above LA and pretend he was already a famous actor making millions of dollars. He wouldn't allow himself to come back down (even if it took all night) until he actually *believed* it.

Give It A Go
Practice *acting as if* on the new thinking, the new beliefs you chose. Make sure you use words that are definite, for example — must, will, absolutely, definitely. Use your voice and body in the way a person would who *absolutely believes* what he/she is saying. You may even want to choose a role model for how to speak and move.

All that is necessary to break the spell of inertia and frustration is this: Act as if it were impossible to fail. That is the talisman, the formula, the command of right-about-face which turns us from failure towards success. *—Dorothea Brande*

5

Take Action

Having strong desire and commitment to realizing your goals is necessary in creating the future of your dreams, but nothing will take the place of action. Now you must *do something*!

When I was thirty-years-old and a hairstylist, I sat down with a piece of paper and a pen and created the perfect job that I wanted to have by the time I was forty. Since I didn't know precisely what job that was, I wrote down the elements. For instance, among other things, I wrote that I wanted to travel, work with people I enjoyed, earn at least $60,000 a year, and be making a positive difference in people's lives. I had no idea what job would give me that but I knew I needed to begin somewhere. So, I signed up for classes at the local community college.

Although I enjoyed most of my classes, I was particularly drawn to communications. At the time, I thought I wanted to pursue a career in Organizational

Communication but through a series of events, I found my path to a career as a speaker/trainer.

Even though I wasn't sure exactly how taking classes would lead me to the future I desired, those early steps got me moving. For my fortieth birthday present, Tony Robbins and his wife, Becky, took me to their island resort in Fiji. There I was — sitting on the beach at age forty, making $75,000 (the goal had been $60,000), traveling the world, working with people I loved and most importantly, making a positive differ- ence in people's lives.

It all begins with the first step. Take action now toward the life you *really* want!

Give It A Go
For the next week, take at least one action each day toward one or more of your goals. An action could be as simple as making a phone call, doing some research, signing up for a class, talking openly about what you are up to, etc. but make sure you are taking forward action. Keep track in your journal.

The vision must be followed by the venture. It is not enough to stare up the steps — we must step up the stairs. —*Vance Havner*

6

Go Until

How many times should you let a baby try walking until you stop them? Easy answer—until they learn to walk. If you really want something badly enough, keep going! There may be times when you feel discouraged but just keep learning from what hasn't worked *and* from what has worked. Be creative, adjust your approach and go again! The main difference between success and failure is perseverance and time.

What if your goal has a time line, like an Olympic Gold Medal by the age of sixteen and you're sixteen and haven't yet accomplished it? You have two choices. Adjust your timeline *or* take all of the great lessons you learned during your pursuit and use those to accomplish your next goal. There are no guarantees in life but great things can happen on the very next try.

My son and I went through three extremely difficult years when he was a teenager. I tried countless things to try to get him back on a track that would lead him to a healthy, happy future. After three years of blood, sweat and tears he finally began to turn his life around. Years later I asked him what the turning point had been for him and his response really surprised me. He said, "Mom, I've thought about this a lot and I really think that the thing that turned me around was when one day I realized that you were never going to f___ing give up! I realized that you were more committed to my success than I was to being bad."

The bottom line is that you must take action toward your dreams, goals and desires. Then, no matter what happens along the path, learn from it, regroup and go again. *If you are willing to persevere, anything is possible!*

Give It A Go
Notice when you have the tendency to quit or give up. When that happens — take one more step forward. Then just keep repeating that process until you reach your destination!

Nothing in the world can take the place of persistence. Talent will not; nothing is more common than unsuccessful men with talent. Genius will not; unrewarded genius is almost a proverb. Education will not; the world is full of educated derelicts. Persistence and determination alone are omnipotent.
—*Calvin Coolidge*

7

Develop Your *Knowing* Muscle

This is a biggie. Some of us have an inner voice, some of us feel it in our bodies, some of us get pictures or visions in our minds. Sometimes we call this intuition, or maybe we say that we are being guided by God or the universe. I don't know precisely what this force is, but I do know that through it, the life of your dreams is at your fingertips.

If you talk to any successful business person, they will tell you that most of their important business decisions were not based solely on the facts but, also on their feelings or intuition. The trick is learning to distinguish between emotions and/or logic, and *your knowing*. Knowing comes from some place deep within you.

We often spend a lot of time procrastinating because we are engulfed in our fears and uncertainties *or* because we are running logical scenarios looking for answers that never seem to come. Sometimes it's the opposite. We blindly jump into situations that are not good for us because we are so excited, or we justify our choices with all of our logical reasons — only to have to pay the consequences later.

How do you develop the ability to consistently *know*? The answer is to practice and stay aware. Have you ever been in a room filled with people talking and, through the noise, you heard and recognized the voice of a friend? You had learned to distinguish that person's voice from all of the other voices. It's the same with developing your "knowing muscle."

The great thing is that the "knowing muscle" is there right now and you already have the ability to access it. All you have to do is let yourself see, hear and feel it more and more each day.

Give It A Go

Write down at least 3-5 times that you felt that sense of "knowing". How did you know? Was it a voice, a feeling, and/or a picture? How did it differ from other voices, feelings and pictures? Increase your awareness and you will continue to get better at recognizing your own *knowing*.

———————◆———————

Wisdom means listening to the still, small voice, the whisper that can be easily lost in the whirlwind of busyness, expectations, and conventions of the world. —*Jean M. Blomquist*

———————◆———————

8

Trust and Follow Your *Knowing*

While it is <u>very important</u> to recognize your *knowing*, there's more to it. Once you *know* what you are being led to do or not do, you must trust and follow through. How many times have you known the right thing and done something else? That behavior was the story of my life. Trusting and following your *knowing* can be tough sometimes but the more you do it, the easier it gets, and the better your life will be.

The way I got myself to begin trusting more was by looking at what a mess I had made of things when I didn't trust, when I ignored my *knowing*. Finally, I thought to myself, "Well, <u>you can't do any worse by beginning to trust and by following your inner voice.</u>" So I just decided to <u>try it</u> — even when it was difficult.

I trusted and followed my inner voice the night I found out that, during a robbery in his store, my father had been shot and was dying. My brother called me late at night and told me I should fly to Arkansas immediately to be with him. While I was shocked and sad, I didn't want to go and I told my brother not to expect me. A few moments after getting off the phone, my inner voice quietly said, "Just go." I decided to trust it and follow so I immediately made my plane reservations for the next morning.

I arrived just in time to be with my father when the respirators were turned off. The experience of being with him when he died changed my life forever. By trusting and following my *knowing*, I had an experience that allowed me to send my father away with love and a peaceful heart and freed me from all the pain I had carried with me my entire life.

Give It A Go
Practice *trusting and following*. Write in your journal times when you "knew" what you should do or not do but you *didn't follow through*. Next write about the times when and you *did follow through*. What did you learn from doing that exercise that will help you trust and follow through more in the future?

———————●———————

...we need to be willing to let our intuition
guide us, and then be willing to follow
that guidance directly and fearlessly.
—J Shakti Gawain

———————●———————

9

Be A Lifetime Learner

One of my friends met Dr. Norman Vincent Peale when he was in his 90s. Dr. Peale wrote one of the first personal development books called, *The Power of Positive Thinking*. My friend said that the first thing he noticed was how alive and full of energy that "old" man was. At one point, during their conversation, Dr. Peale excitedly exclaimed, "There's just so much to learn."

Contrast that with some people who have that lifeless, deadpan look on their faces. They often times think they know everything — they've seen it all. Or think about some relationships where you feel like you know everything about the other person — boring! Thinking we know everything about anything is an illusion, and it can be a dangerous one.

Have you ever seen the joy of discovery on a child's face? Learning keeps you vibrant, alive, interested (and interesting). Whatever you want, continuing to learn and grow can only help. Learn more about yourself and the people close to you. Learn new skills related to your work; learn a new language; learn to use the latest technology; learn how to cook; learn to dance (it lifts the spirit)...

My personal goal is to be just like Dr. Peale when I'm in my 90s. I'll be talking with my great grandchildren about something new they are doing and I will exclaim, "There's just so much to learn!"

Give It A Go
Get started. Think of something you've said or even thought would be fun to learn and get going on it. Sign up for a class, start reading a book on the subject or ask someone to start teaching you. Jump in with both feet and have fun learning!

The illiterate of the 21st century will not be those who cannot read and write, but those who cannot learn, unlearn, and relearn.
—Alvin Toffler

36

10

Associate With
Positive Energy Givers

The people we surround ourselves with are very, very important to the kind of experiences we have. While I'm a big believer in the necessity of taking responsibility for our own lives, our own successes and happiness, it would be foolish to ignore the fact that the people around us play a part in how we handle life. If we spend time with people who believe in us, love us, encourage us and infuse us with positive energy and spirit, we will be lifted higher.

When I first began my journey toward creating the life I really wanted, I attended several seminars. It was there that I began to realize how important it was to be around people who would support my dreams, believe in me even when I didn't and help keep me focused on what was really important. Of course, I did the same for them. Doing that also reinforced the new thinking I was developing. Could I have done it all on my own? Maybe, but I'm not convinced I would have gone as far, as fast without that network of positive energy givers. There are probably some people you can think of in your life that make you feel better about yourself and life by just being around them. Hang on to those people! Cherish them and make sure you give them the same.

Other times you may notice that there are some people who practically suck the energy and spirit right out of you. Of course, everyone has bad days and I'm not suggesting that you dump your friends because they are not always "up". I'm not suggesting your abandon your husband or wife because they are going through a rough time. There will always be times when you will need to be the one who infuses others with your positive energy, love, encouragement, and spirit!

Make the conscious choice to be with people who encourage you to feel good about yourself, your abilities and your life. Seek out people who inspire you to be a better person.

Give It A Go
Take stock. Do you have enough people in your life who infuse you with positive energy? If yes - go give them a big hug and a thank you! If no, begin adding new people in, and if absolutely necessary, make the decision to spend less time (or no time) with the people who are consistently negative energy drains. Create a network of energy givers!

———————◆———————

Surround yourself with only people who are going to lift you higher. —*Oprah Winfrey*

———————◆———————

38

11

Treasure And Nurture Your Friends

Friendship is one of the most important relationships we can have. Good friends stay with us through good times and bad times. They are there to share our excitement when something wonderful happens and also there to support us through difficult situations and heartache. With them, we can laugh, cry, look stupid, brag, be weak, be strong — it's all okay.

Like anything else worthwhile, friends require nurturing, maintenance and love. The bottom line is that to reap the rewards of security, love, fun, freedom to be yourself, trust, laughter, and companionship, you have to invest something of yourself. Learning to be a good friend is one of the greatest benefits of all.

Do you ever get so busy with your own life that you forget to take time to nurture your friendships? Be careful. Don't call on your friends only when you need something. It's common for people to ignore their friends when their lives are busy and full and then expect them to be there when they are having problems or are lonely. It doesn't work that way.

As I write this, two amazing women that I've been friends with since fifth grade are sleeping in the other room. They flew up from Mississippi and Tennessee to spend the weekend with me (we make it a point to see each other at least once a year). Imagine! We met when we were twelve and through all the years, we've remained friends! This last couple of days, we have laughed, reminisced, solved each other's problems, planned for the future, and been grateful for the knowledge that we have one another in our lives.

Great friendships require an investment of attention, time, energy, love and support but the rewards are priceless!

Give It A Go
This week do something special for a friend or two. Let them know you love them. Surprise them with something that they would really enjoy, share more of yourself with them, help them with a project... Most importantly, make time for old and new friendships!

———————————•———————————

Friendship is the only cement that will ever hold the world together. *—Woodrow Wilson*

———————————•———————————

12

Get Out Of Your Comfort Zone

Since we are human beings, <u>we are predisposed to seek comfort</u>. There is nothing wrong with enjoying your life and creating a comfortable environment — with this caveat — <u>make sure your comfort doesn't become a hindrance for growth.</u>

Let's use this metaphor: If you want to grow your muscles, what must you do? That's right, you must tax them regularly. You can't go to the gym once and then say, "whew, glad that's over." You also can't do what most people do, which is stop when it gets a little difficult. Any bodybuilder knows that it's the two or three reps *after* they start to feel pressure when the real growth begins. They know that pushing beyond the point of discomfort (not pain) is the true key.

I'm a big believer in balance. Sometimes it's fun to enjoy where you are; stay at the top of the mountain you've climbed and enjoy the view. But if you stay there too long, you can miss many other great experiences. Since I first decided to create an *E Ticket Life*, I've been regularly pushing the edge of my comfort zone.

When I first moved to New York City, I received an email from a friend about an audition for a new off/off Broadway play about Tango. The idea of auditioning was scary but it seemed like it might be fun, and I was in New York, afterall. I decided to go for it. That week was excruciatingly difficult. I had butterflies in my stomach; I practiced a monologue for hours (with an accent no less); I tried on tons of outfits; I called friends for help and then I did it. I auditioned for the first time in my life at the age of forty-nine! No, I didn't get the part but I did get a second audition.

Get out of *your* comfort zone and enjoy the ride!

Give It A Go
Do something this week that you've been putting off because it's outside your comfort zone. Write down how you feel now — before you do it. Then step out there and go for it! Notice and write down how you feel afterwards. What else have you been thinking about but not doing? Make getting out of your comfort zone a regular part of your life.

It is not because things are difficult that we do not dare, it is because we do not dare that they are difficult. —*Seneca*

13

Don't Take Yourself Too Seriously —
Especially When You're Emotional

Learning this lesson has helped me cut down on bad decisions and has helped me have a lot more fun. I became aware of the importance of this during my first career as a hairstylist. I would frequently encounter situations like this: A woman with long hair would come in saying, "Cut it off; I want it all off!" In my early, inexperienced days I would take them seriously and cut it all off. Afterwards, I had to deal with an unhappy client moaning, "Oh my God, what have I done? Why did you let me do that?"

After one or two of those experiences, when a client came in exclaiming "Cut it all off", I responded, "OK, what's going on?" Often the person had just had a fight with or broken up with a boyfriend or husband. I learned to distinguish between someone making a decision out of *high emotion* versus it being something they *really* wanted. I began telling them, "I'll cut it all off but, not now. If you *still* want to cut your hair short next week, *then* I'll do it but not while you are in this

43

state of mind." I learned not to take their decisions too seriously while they were in a state of high emotion.

The trick was transferring this learning into my own life. I began to notice that when I was upset I would concoct all sorts of additional problems. I could turn a simple situation into a full-blown disaster within a matter of moments. Other times I would get very excited about something and I was off and running without giving it a thought. It was easy for me to think or believe that what I was feeling in the moment was the *truth* and that often resulted in bad decisions. Fortunately, I learned to consciously choose not to take myself too seriously in those instances. I began treating myself like I had my clients.

Learn to put off any serious decisions until you're in a centered, relaxed state of mind.

Give It A Go
Decide now not to take yourself and your thinking too seriously when you are in any high emotional state of mind. Check in after the dust has settled to find your real truth and remember — emotions can change with the wind, your truth is quiet, solid and leads you to your greatest good.

He who controls others may be powerful, but he who has mastered himself is mightier still.
—*Lao-Tzu*

14

Genuinely Thank People — Often

One morning after breakfast my friend and I were leaving the hotel where we were staying during a business trip. As we walked past the gentleman at the front desk, my friend exclaimed, "Bjorn, you are my hero! Thank you so much for fixing the heater last night!" He beamed a smile from ear to ear and uttered a shy, "You're welcome." When we were outside, I said, "What was that all about? Don't you think calling him a hero for just doing his job is a little excessive?" She looked a little puzzled and said, "No, he really is my hero. I'm grateful that he quickly handled the problem so I could snuggle up for the night in my nice warm room."

I used to think it was unnecessary to thank people for simply "doing their jobs" or for doing what was expected of them. Why thank my son for taking out the trash — he's supposed to. Someone would have had to do something extraordinary for me to actually stop, feel grateful and then thank them. My perception caused me to miss many opportunities to make someone feel good and to have more fun myself.

45

In order to genuinely thank someone, first we have to *feel appreciative*. When we feel appreciative, it radiates through our hearts, minds and bodies. When I began to consciously look for things to appreciate in people, in life and in challenging situations, the world around me started to take on a new richness.

It gets even better when you take the next step and *express your gratitude outwardly*. Have you ever eagerly waited to give someone a present that you knew they would love? Remember what it felt like when they gave you a big thank you hug. Doesn't it feel great to know that something you've done has made someone else happy? When you genuinely thank people, not only do you fill yourself up but you also get to give the other person the gift of knowing they've made a difference. It's a great, positive cycle.

Give It A Go
For the next week, genuinely thank at least one person a day (preferably more) using this two-part formula.

1) Thank them for something and make sure you are specific.
2) Tell them *why* you appreciate it so much.

You'll both enjoy a great ride!

When someone does something good, applaud!
You will make two people happy.
—*Samuel Goldwyn*

15

Lighten Up

My daughter had to go to the doctor for some shots before a trip she was taking to Costa Rica. At the office, she saw a very, very old woman. It was then that she had, what I call, a *moment of clarity*. There are many other ways to describe these moments — the light bulb went off, an insight, an "ah ha"...

She called me later to tell me about her *moment of clarity.* "Mom, I realized something today. *You* are going to get old and then you are going to die. (Great — thanks a lot for reminding me of that!) *I'm* going to get old and then I'm going to die. *Everyone* is going to die." The odd thing was that she didn't sound depressed about this realization. On the contrary, she sounded almost happy. She continued, "No, really, I don't mean it in a bad way. It's not a bad thing; it's just that we only have one chance to live this life. What I realized today is that we shouldn't take everything so seriously. Most of the things we get upset about just aren't that important."

Is your child spilling his milk *really* that big of a deal? Of course not! Besides, when you are yelling at your child for spilling the milk, you miss the opportunity to look into his/her little face and see the fear (confusion or embarrassment — whatever). You miss the chance to smile, give him/her a hug, scoot them off to get paper towels and just clean it up. You miss the opportunity to teach them that mistakes are not only okay, but a fact of life.

When something isn't going the way you want it to, say oops or oh well, and then *move on* to making it the way you want it. Life is too short to waste precious time making mountains out of molehills. So make like the angels and *lighten up* — on yourself and others.

Give It A Go
Practice incorporating "oops" and "oh well" into your day. Look for the humor or opportunity in situations that usually upset you. Check out the wonderful book, *Don't Sweat The Small Stuff and It's All Small Stuff* by Richard Carlson, PhD.

Mix a little foolishness with your serious plans:
it's lovely to be silly at the right moment.
—*Horace*

16

Listen

There are some lessons I'm still learning and this is one of them. I'm such a talker but as I continue to improve in this area, my life becomes richer and fuller. There are so many reasons to listen more that I hardly know where to begin. Here are a few that stand out.

Listening...

➤ Shows support and caring to the people you love
➤ Makes people feel accepted, valued and respected
➤ Allows you to clear up misconceptions
➤ Helps you understand what's important to other people
➤ Is a great resource when you want to persuade
➤ Encourages other people to say what they think/feel
➤ Let's you share in someone else's joy and excitement
➤ Builds bonds with people
➤ Makes *you* come across like a great conversationalist
➤ Helps avoid (or more quickly end) arguments
➤ Can save you from costly mistakes in business
➤ Helps you learn many interesting things
➤ Can be a lot of fun

As a child, the single greatest hurt I experienced in my relationship with my mother was the feeling of not being listened to. I can contrast that with the tremendous love and peace I felt with my favorite aunt. She always listened and I felt like she listened with her heart as well as her ears.

It's interesting that, even though this is something that I experienced growing up, I would still talk too much and listen too little in my own adult life. Fortunately, I have recognized this tendency and I'm now getting to enjoy the wondrous experiences that listening more brings.

In what areas of your life do you need to listen more attentively?

Give It A Go
Practice being an active listener. Ask more questions and really listen to the answers with your heart, as well as your mind. Have fun learning and notice the impact you are having on others when you actually listen.

A good listener is not only popular everywhere,
but after a while he knows something.
—*Wilson Mizner Churchill Mackay*

17

Smile A Lot

When I was younger, I didn't smile much and I didn't even realize it. Although, my first clue should have been how often people would say to me, "Smile, it's not that bad." They probably said this to try to make me smile, which of course, didn't work. Instead, I was irritated because I felt fine — or so I thought. One day I became curious as to why I heard this so often and I began to pay attention to my smiling (or lack thereof).

I was astounded at how rarely I smiled. I had become a master of the deadpan look. I even explored where this came from and realized that I had sort of inherited it from my father. Even though he was from a small town in Arkansas, he was like the quintessential mafia Godfather. Through a simple look, my father could make a person an offer he/she couldn't refuse. Likewise, most of his jokes were delivered in that same, deadpan way.

I decided that it was something worth changing because I didn't want to be seen that way by others. More importantly, I didn't want to be that way for myself. As odd as this sounds, at first it felt unnatural to smile. I was accustomed to only smiling when I was really, really happy. So, smiling when just saying hello to someone practically hurt my face. But I practiced smiling and my life improved in several ways...

➤ I began to feel more relaxed and comfortable
➤ My image of myself changed
➤ More people smiled at me
➤ Things that I used to be afraid to do became more fun
➤ I noticed more people told me I was pretty
➤ I felt happier

Give It A Go
This week, smile at least 25-50% more than usual — (try it even if you're already a "smiler"). Smile at people on the street, at your children, while you are getting dressed in the morning, while you are lying in bed before you go to sleep — smile for no particular reason! Notice how much better you feel in general and notice the difference in the way people react to you.

———————◆———————

Smile at each other; smile at your wife, smile at your husband, smile at your children, smile at each other—it doesn't matter who it is—and that will help you to grow up in greater love for each other. —*Mother Teresa Of Calcutta*

———————◆———————

18

Practice Abundance Thinking

Abundance thinking is when a person believes that there is plenty. Plenty of love, plenty of money, plenty of happiness, plenty of goodness, plenty of health, plenty, plenty, plenty... Scarcity thinking is when a person believes there is a limit, a scarce supply of everything. Scarcity of love, scarcity of money, scarcity of happiness, scarcity of goodness, scarcity, scarcity, scarcity...

I think I first began to understand the power of abundance thinking when I was the manager for a team of sales people. I observed time and time again how the salespeople who believed there were plenty of customers for everyone (including competitors) consistently had higher sales numbers than the people who focused on the scarcity of prospects. This happened even when the *abundance thinkers* actually had fewer appointments set for them than the *scarcity thinkers*.

We will tend to see and experience whatever we focus on. The salespeople who focused on abundance were creatively finding new sources of customers and referrals. The ones who focused on scarcity spent an exorbitant amount of time worrying, complaining and, through their lack of action, *proving* their belief that there wasn't enough to go around was "true."

Sometimes it's hard to believe in abundance when the physical evidence suggest limits. So often we want to see it *before* we will believe it. But as Dr. Wayne Dyer's book title says — *You'll See It When You Believe It.*

I highly encourage everyone to practice *abundance thinking*. The more worried you are about something you feel is lacking in your life, the more important it is that you *change your thinking*. When you truly let go of your scarcity thinking and the fear that usually comes with it, you'll find the thing you desire beginning to flow easily and effortlessly into your life.

Give It A Go

Write down any and all areas where you have a fear or a belief that there's not enough. Be willing to let that thinking go now and begin believing there is plenty. Start looking for the abundance. Keep notes in your journal of what you are noticing. The more you look for it, the more you will find it.

Put aside the idea that there is not enough
to go around. —*Barrie Dolnick*

19

Do The Right Thing

Several years ago I had the pleasure of hearing General Norman Schwarzkopf speak on leadership. One of his fundamental messages was, <u>when in doubt, do the right thing!</u> Simple? Sure. Easy? Not always.

I believe that I built my entire business as a successful hairstylist based on that principle. When I first started cutting hair, I didn't have much money and I had two small children to take care of. I began working in a new town and I didn't know anyone or have a base of clients. I paid $50 a week for my babysitter and $60 a week to rent my booth. Here's the kicker. In those early months, there were weeks when I only made $80 or $90 dollars — you do the math.

At that time, we used to charge $55 for a "perm" which was half of my weekly nut. But what do you do when someone comes in waving (metaphorically anyway) $55 dollars at you and you know that a perm will destroy their already damaged hair? As tough as it was, I discouraged them from getting the process done. Why? Simple. It was the right thing to do. It wasn't always easy but it actually paid off in the long run. I built a great business on my referrals.

Often when a referral came to me for the first time, they would tell me that they were there because their friend had said that they could count on me to tell them the truth.

How do you know what the right thing is? It's easy really. It's the thing you would do if you had no fear, no anger, no frustration. It's the thing you know, in your heart of hearts, is right. I know it can be very difficult when you fear having someone yell at you, you're worried about losing a job or you're afraid of any of the many other possible consequences. Although, I'm sure you'll find that doing the right thing pays off in the long run and is worth the risk.

Give It A Go
From now on do the right thing. Practice doing it especially when you are afraid, angry, frustrated... You may have to summon some extra courage but you'll be glad you did and it will get easier and easier each time!

Cowardice asks the question, Is it safe?
Expediency asks the question, Is it politic?
Vanity asks the question, Is it popular? But
conscience asks the question, Is it right?
And there comes a time when one must
take a position that is neither safe, nor
politic, nor popular, but he must take it
because his conscience tells him it is
right... —*Martin Luther King, Jr.*

20

Give Lots Of Compliments

Many years ago, someone told me, "If you think something nice about someone or something — shout it from the highest rooftop. If you think something bad — keep it to yourself."

In order to give lots of great compliments, *you have to be looking for things to compliment*. Interestingly, doing that can increase *your* enjoyment of life. Also, by not just thinking the nice things but also saying them, you get to help someone else have an *E Ticket Day*. Plus you may find that giving compliments has unexpected and fun side benefits...

When I was in Amsterdam giving a seminar, I went to dance Tango one evening and saw a couple dancing who was amazing! I wanted to tell them how great they were but I felt a little shy about going over and saying it. Finally, I jumped in and walked over to tell them they were fabulous dancers. When I did, one of them said to me, "Is your name Debra?" Well, you could have knocked me over with a feather because I didn't know anyone in Amsterdam! Cautiously, I answered with a confused, "Yes." It turns out that they were friends with someone I knew who was living in Rome. My friend knew I was going to be in Amsterdam and had told them to look out for me when they went to dance Tango. Because of that one compliment, I was able to meet up with my friend in Rome and have another great adventure!

Here's a great formula for giving a compliment:

1. Simply state the compliment.
2. Back it up with a detail or reason for saying it. *This gives more weight to the compliment.*
3. Ask a question that engages the person. *This helps eliminate that awkward moment that sometimes happens after a compliment.*

For instance: You are so fun to be around. Every time I see you, I laugh and I always leave feeling great. Are you just naturally fun or did you develop this ability to make people feel good?

Give It A Go
Give at least one genuine compliment every day for a week and try using this formula. Here's a hint — make the compliments deeper than, "nice tie." People like to get compliments related to their skills, their personality, their intelligence, their good taste, their efforts... Have fun with it!

Compliments invite the person who is compli-
mented to embrace a new perception of him or
herself. And just as layers and layers of nacre
form a pearl over an irritating grain of sand, so
compliments collect around us, developing us in
all our beauty. *—Daphne Rose Kingma*

21

Be Willing To Be Wrong

If you are anything like me, you enjoy being right. You may have noticed by now that I have no problem expressing my opinions on a lot of things but thinking I'm always right is a limitation that, in the past, prevented me from fully experiencing my *E Ticket Life*.

The real message here is this: <u>stay open to other possibilities and perspectives other than what you believe to be true</u>. Granted, whatever you think or believe, you think or believe those things for a reason. We usually have a long list of evidence or experiences that support why something is true for us. This is one of the reasons we often have such a difficult time considering other possibilities.

The other day I was reading the book, *The Art Of Happiness* by the Dalai Lama. There was a section in which the co-author, Howard C. Cutler, M.D. challenged the validity (at least in today's world) of a prayer, from the eleventh century, that the Dalai Lama recites.

Keep in mind that this is a prayer that he meditates on daily so it is obviously at the core of his beliefs. According to Dr. Cutler, when challenged on it, the Dalai Lama stopped for several moments and then acknowledged the other man's perspective. He did this by discussing, in detail, situations where the insights in the prayer might need modification. Even though I wasn't there, I was enthralled by the Dalai Lama's willingness to reevaluate a cherished position. I also realize that other "true" masters I've met seem to share this willingness to look at things with fresh eyes.

When we are willing to be wrong; when we are willing to consider different thinking about ourselves, each other, our work, what's possible... a whole world opens up to us. That new world may help us to more quickly resolve a disagreement with a loved one or help us find solutions to difficult dilemmas in our work. In the world outside of our current thinking, there are insights that could change our lives in dramatic and wonderful ways.

Give It A Go
Notice when you begin to defend your position on anything. Stop and genuinely consider another person's position or perspective. How else could you look at it? What are some other possibilities?

Let go of your attachment to being right, and suddenly your mind is more open. You're able to benefit from the unique viewpoints of others, without being crippled by your own judgment.
—Ralph Marston

22

Like Yourself

Don't you love those adorable little children who run around bragging about their finger paintings, their delicious mud pies or their singing? It's so cute the way they take such genuine pleasure in themselves. Having a positive self-image is usually a simple matter for very young children who haven't yet been influenced by the external world. Unfortunately, somewhere along the way many people begin to feel like they are not good enough, smart enough, rich enough, thin enough — or the opposite happens. A person's self-image can become inflated and they begin to think they are better than everyone else.

How can you rediscover the natural ability to like yourself? One way is simple — *stop comparing yourself to anyone else to decide how to feel about you.* The problem with comparison in creating your own self-image is two-fold. If you are constantly focused on people who you perceive as better than you or more fortunate than you — be prepared to feel badly about yourself a lot. There will always be someone like that out there. On the other hand, be careful about swinging the pendulum and looking for people to feel superior to in order to boost your own self-image. Doing that separates you from people and can prevent you from learning and growing. Either way, comparing yourself to others to determine your own self worth is a vicious cycle that is always driven by external factors.

Each person is unique and wonderful. Each person in this world has qualities, skills and talents that can be appreciated and enjoyed. The more one learns to appreciate oneself (minus the comparisons), the easier it is to see and appreciate other people for their special qualities. That also can be a cycle – but is a positive one driven from within.

Give It A Go
Make a list of all the things you like about yourself. Make sure none of them even hint of comparison. For instance, I'm a good listener vs. I'm a better listener than most people. Have fun with this. Anytime you notice something, write it down. Become your own greatest admirer and remember to balance that with admiring the people around you as well.

Nobody will think you're somebody if you don't think so yourself. —*African-American proverb*

23

Be A Positive Belief Collector

This has been one of my favorite hobbies for years. I love to listen to people's beliefs and then collect or choose the ones that I think would be great for me to have. Since we are collecting beliefs all the time anyway, we may as well do it in a more conscious way and choose the ones that will help us create the life we *really* want.

So I listen. I hear people say things like — "Life is hard." REJECT! "It's difficult to meet people." REJECT! "You can't trust anyone these days." REJECT! "The world is a scary place!" REJECT!

Everyday in the news, on the street, at work and in our own minds, beliefs like the ones listed above are thrown out there. Take control of what happens next. *It's your choice to accept or reject those beliefs.* The question is, based on what criteria? Some people say that you should base your beliefs on what is true but truth is a perception — a focus. Consider this cycle: what we believe directs the actions we take, the actions we take lead us to certain outcomes or results. If you believe the world is hard, I promise you — it will be. If you believe the world is a fabulous playground, then even if things are difficult around you, you'll find a way to make the most of it.

I listen to the beliefs of people who are clearly living lives they love. "Everyday above ground is a great day!" ACCEPTED! "When you're skating on thin ice, you might as well dance!" ACCEPTED! "Everyone loves me, and if they don't at first, then they will when they get to know me!" ACCEPTED! "There is always a way if I'm committed!" ACCEPTED! "True spirituality is a mental attitude that you can practice at any moment." ACCEPTED! "Life is a joy and it's fun to be alive!" ACCEPTED! "I create money quickly and easily!" ACCEPTED! These are just a few of the beliefs that, through the years, I have added to my treasured collection.

Give It A Go
Start your own positive belief collection. List the positive beliefs you already have. Then begin adding new ones you hear or read that could help you reach your goals. Take those new ones and try them on for a week (or a lifetime).

Here's one more for your "collection." To believe that what has not occurred in history will not occur at all is to argue disbelief in the dignity of man. —*Mahatma Ghandhi*

24

Embrace Your Problems

Try this: put your palms together and with your right palm PUSH against your left. Did you do it? Here's the question, when you pushed with your right palm, did you automatically push back with your left? Almost everyone I've ever done this with answers — yes. When we resist anything, the tendency is for that thing to persist or push back.

Most of us tend to resist, to push against the things we don't like in our lives, our problems. The more we push, the more they tend to push back. As odd as it may sound, see what happens when you begin to embrace, accept, even appreciate your problems. My experience is that problems are potentially great gifts in disguise. Granted, some of them are more cleverly disguised than others.

I heard a quote once that, in essence, said: The only people free of problems can be found in the grave-yards. Therefore, a common sense approach to dealing with something that will always be there (in one form or another) is to <u>make the most of it </u> — don't ya think? It will take willingness and probably some practice to consistently look for and find the opportunities and benefits that come disguised as problems.

Embracing our problems allows us to find solutions more quickly, helps us recognize opportunities and lets the stress and negative energy of the situations ease away more gently.

When I was responsible for all of the live events for Tony Robbins, we were planning a large seminar in Los Angeles. Five weeks before the event, there was a devastating earthquake centered near the planned location. The city was at a standstill and people were emotionally reeling. We could have decided to cancel. Instead, we looked for opportunities to use the program to help the people in Los Angeles. We found many creative ways to be of service to the community and still managed to have a successful event.

We can be thrown a curve at anytime in life. Work with it, rather than against it and anything is possible.

Give It A Go
Write down some of your problems and play with the idea of being grateful for them. Then ask yourself questions like: What is the opportunity here? What's potentially good about this? How can I make this work for me? How can I work with (rather than against) this situation?

Bad times have a scientific value. These are
occasions a good learner would not miss.
—*Ralph Waldo Emerson*

25

Let Go Of Regrets

When I first made the decision to make my life an E Ticket Ride, I also made a commitment to myself to live a life that is regret free. At first I thought that the only way to do that would be to always live in perfect harmony with my *knowing* and to never make any more bad decisions in my life. In the many years since I made the choice of how I wanted to live, I still believe it's important to strive for that harmony with my *knowing* and to make good decisions. But that's not always going happen.

A few years ago, I was working in a job that was very challenging for me. Nevertheless, it was a great period of growth, skill development, making friends, strengthening my confidence and many other positive benefits. There was a point, though, where I knew it was time to go and I didn't. I stayed for one more year and that year was exceptionally difficult. When I did finally make the decision to move on, it would have been very easy for me to have regretted staying longer than I felt I should have. It would have been easy for me to berate myself for not having trusted and followed my intuition. But I realized that there was absolutely no point in regretting something that was done and in the past. Instead, I became grateful for receiving the lesson (one more time) that ignoring my *knowing* has consequences that are often painful. I also believe that maybe I needed to get that lesson, yet again, to prepare me for some future decision. Either way, I learned from it, let go of the regret and moved on.

People will ask me if I regret getting married three times. The answer is no, I do not. I'm sure there could have been easier ways to make my way through life but I have wonderful children, I love who I have become and the life I have now. Every experience I've had is part of the tapestry that makes me who I am so why regret anything in my past. What regrets do you need to let go of now?

Give It A Go
Write down any regrets you have in your life. Then also write down what you've learned, how you have become a better person, who you've met or what great things have happened as a result. At the very least, be grateful that you learned not to do that again. Keep the value and let the regret go!

———————◆———————

Things without all remedy should be without regard; what's done is done.
—*William Shakespeare*

———————◆———————

26

Understand Lag Time

We live in a world where most people want, even expect, instant gratification. If they aren't getting it, it's common for people to move on to the next thing. As a result, many people never stick with anything long enough to benefit from achieving the result they were after initially.

Lag time is the time that exists between the actions we take and the ultimate result or consequence. For instance, when we first begin to eat more healthy or start exercising, there is some period of time that will lapse before we see the results. On the other hand, if we stop eating well and working out, there will be some period of time before we see the consequences of that behavior. Often times, we don't get immediate gratification for doing the right thing and we don't experience immediate consequences for doing the wrong thing.

Understanding lag time helps a person continue doing things in the direction of their goals even when it doesn't appear that their efforts are paying off. The main thing is to make the necessary adjustments in what you are doing along the way without giving up. Depending on the situation, lag time could be a few minutes or it could be a few years.

When my son turned fifteen, he started on a path that could have had negative, lifetime consequences for him. I was committed to helping him change paths so that he could become a happy, healthy adult. It was difficult but I understood that I had to keep doing everything I could, even though it didn't *seem* to be working. I had faith that we would make it through and I never stopped doing the things that I thought would help. Eventually, he made the turnaround and is now a wonderfully insightful, kind, healthy, and happy man. *The bottom line is — stick with it!*

Give It A Go
Start to notice when you feel like quitting because you aren't getting what you want *yet*. Hang in there and keep doing what you know is right. Eventually you'll be rewarded.

Look at a stone cutter hammering away at his rock, perhaps a hundred times without as much as a crack showing in it. Yet at the hundred-and-first blow it will split in two, and I know it was not the last blow that did it, but all that had gone before. —*Jacob A. Riis*

84

27

Feel The Negative Feelings
Then *Move On*

During my early days in the seminar world, I learned a lesson that has lasted ever since and I'm very grateful for it. During that time, I was learning how to "manage my state of mind" which is a very valuable skill. Unfortunately though, I was beginning to think that "managing my state" meant that I should never feel bad.

The first time I was a team leader at a big, two-week seminar, of course I wanted to do a great job. I had been working sixteen hour days and I was exhausted. Suddenly I was faced with an angry participant who had disliked me from the beginning and she let me know that she thought I was the worst team leader ever. Well, I was crushed and as soon as she walked away I began to sob.

Three of the top people from the seminar (separately) came over and tried to get me to "change my state." I would stop crying in that moment and as soon as they walked away, I would start crying again. Finally, one of the staff members (supposedly not trained in how to deal with people) came over and asked me a magical question, "What do you need?" I looked at him and said, "I think I just need to cry." We went outside, I put my head on his shoulder and I cried for about five minutes. Afterwards, I felt so much better and then I was able to focus on what to do next and how to resolve the situation with the woman.

Of course, if crying every time someone was unhappy with me had become a pattern, I would've found a way to change my response. Nevertheless, denying, suppressing or resisting one's feelings doesn't solve anything. *Remember, what we resist, persist.*

Give It A Go

Give yourself permission to feel your emotions. Then if there are some that you would like to change, great, change them. Learn to move past your feelings rather than denying them. All feelings have their place and can serve you.

...when we keep negative feelings out of sight, they smother the love that seems to lie deeper and closer to the real self. —*Elizabeth O'Connor*

28

Be More Curious

Who are the most alive people on the earth? Children! Watch a little child sometime. They are fully "present" and immersed in this wonderful experience of life. One of the things that makes them so involved is their insatiable curiosity. Little children are rarely bored because their curiosity kicks in and they can become fascinated with the smallest thing. Are you ever bored with your job, your spouse, your friends, your city or yourself? Curiosity cures boredom. Do people find you boring? Curiosity can cure that, too.

I noticed that I was having a difficult time connecting with people as consistently as I wanted to and I couldn't figure out what the problem was. I decided to *model* someone who was (and still is) very good in this area. One of my best friends in the world, Mimi, is a beautiful social butterfly and everyone loves her! So I decided to adopt her beliefs about social interaction with people. What I discovered when I began to explore her beliefs was that when she meets someone, she's curious about them, their life, what's important to them, what makes them tick... While we were talking, I realized that I often didn't have that same level of curiosity.

I decided right then and there to become more curious everyday about people — even those close to me. It was a miracle! I started enjoying people and life in an entirely new way. I also found out that the more interested I was in other people, the more interesting they found me.

Curiosity also assists you in finding solutions to difficult problems, gives you understanding and perspective during arguments, helps you be more creative and generally makes life more fun and interesting.

Give It A Go

Put on your curiosity hat this week. Start wondering about things. Who have you been taking for granted? At work, what have you just accepted as "the way it is?" Why do you respond negatively when... happens? Write down what you learn that you never knew before and any other insights you have from being more curious.

I have no special talents. I am only
passionately curious. —*Albert Einstein*

29

Challenge Your Meanings

I had found them! The shoes I'd been searching for were finally on my feet. I spent way too much money but since I wear a size four (which is very hard to find), I grabbed them. When I arrived at my friend's house, as a courtesy, I took my shoes off at the door. Upon leaving, I couldn't find them. Why? Because it turns out his dog had taken them out to the back yard and chewed them to bits. I couldn't believe it when I saw my new shoes in shreds. What I was even more upset about was my friend's response which was only, "That silly dog." That was it! No apology, nothing.

I was so upset that I didn't dare say anything. I got in my car and drove away thinking... "He's an idiot, he doesn't care about anything, no — worse, he cares more about that stupid dog than he does about his friends" and on and on. Then I stopped and asked myself this question: *"Is this how I want to feel* about my friend?" My answer was "No!" Even though it was very difficult, given my state of mind, I made myself ask the following questions: "What else *could* this mean? How else *could* I look at this?" I got two answers that helped me change how I felt, *"He charges $350 an hour for business consulting and he's been helping me for free for almost two hours so the shoes are a small price to pay. Besides, one of the things I like most about him is how calm and easy going he always is — I can't fault him for being his sweet, laid-back self."* I felt so much better and I was able to quickly let it go. End of story: on a whim, I drove straight to Nordstrom where I had bought the shoes, and miraculously — they replaced them for free!

Whenever something occurs, you automatically attach a meaning to what just happened. This process started when you were a small child and has continued throughout your life, but it's never too late to challenge your meanings. You can even *attach new meanings to your past experiences* — meanings that will empower you to realize your goals and outcomes. And remember to ask this question often as you go through life: *What else could this mean?*

Give It A Go

In your journal, write down some situations that usually make you feel a way you don't want to. Ask yourself how you would prefer to feel when that situation occurs. Then brainstorm (and write down) as many different or possible meanings you can until you come up with a few that will allow you to feel the way you want to. Find meanings that will also help you reach your goals and outcomes. Make it a game — it can be fun!

How we see and hold the full range of our
experiences in our minds and in our hearts
makes an enormous difference in the quality of
this journey we are on, and what it means to us.
It can influence where we go, what happens,
what we learn, and how we feel along the way.
—JonKabat-Zinn

30

Laugh And Play

I know we are all grown up and we have responsi-bilities in our jobs and with our families. But, come on... That doesn't mean we can't have some fun! Laughing and playing is natural. As a child we all had a natural ability to delight in small things, to experi-ment and play — and above all — the ability to laugh!

You may be saying, "Well that was fine when I was a child, but I don't have time for laughing and playing now. Life's tough and I have to work." (or something along those lines). That may be the most important reason of all to laugh and play. According to Doug Hall, author of *Jump Start Your Brain,* you can increase your brainpower three to fivefold simply by laughing and having fun before working on a problem.

The most obvious reason to laugh and play is to increase your happiness but if it helps, there are other more logical reasons. It's been said that laughter is the best medicine. Consider these physiological and psychological benefits to indulging in a little laughter:

Laughter...

- ✈ Strengthens your immune system
- ✈ Enhances your cardio-vascular flexibility
- ✈ Helps you think more clearly
- ✈ Replenishes your creative juices
- ✈ Can release and transform emotional pain
- ✈ Rebalances chemicals in your body
- ✈ Connects people

In my dealings with people from all walks of life, I've seen a widespread inability to have fun. Some people are so out of practice that they can't even enjoy their free time or their vacations. That's so sad. The ability to laugh and play is inherently within each of us so, let go and have some fun!

Give It A Go
For one week find something—anything—to laugh about at least twice a day. If you can't find anything to laugh about, then just laugh for absolutely no good reason. You know how. Just do it. Wake up in the morning and have a good chuckle before you get out of bed and make sure you have a good laugh before you go to sleep. You'll thank me for this one!

———•———

The most wasted of all days is that on which one has not laughed. *—Nicolas Chamfort*

———•———

31

Be Courageous

Fear is a factor in everyone's life. Some people are afraid of adventurous things like extreme sports such as skydiving — others thrive on that. Some people shrink back at the idea of true intimacy while others don't know any other way to relate to people. Supposedly, the number one fear in the world for people is public speaking and then there are those, like me, that you have to drag off the stage. Fear is a natural part of being alive but so is fear's antidote: **courage.**

Eleanor Roosevelt said, "I believe that anyone can conquer fear by doing things he fears to do." But why should we conquer fear? Why not just avoid those things we are fearful of doing? Well, maybe you should. I'm not saying you need to run out and do every single thing you are afraid of doing. But if something inside you wants to be, do, have and/or create something different, there is a good chance you'll need to get beyond some level of fear to make it happen. That could range from being mildly nervous to scared out of your wits. It doesn't matter. You already have the courage you need to break through. You've demonstrated your courage hundreds, if not thousands, of times in your life. As a child, you courageously took those first steps. You got through school, went on first dates, and showed up at that first day at work. Sure, some of you may sometimes have easier access to your courage than others, but the ability to be courageous is within you.

The exciting thing about courage is that, with use, it strengthens. Each small fear you conquer, builds a reserve which will give you greater ability to conquer larger challenges. As you grow, learn, stretch and pursue the life of your dreams — courage will be your best friend.

Give It A Go
Pick 3-5 things that, just thinking of, makes you feel a little nervous or afraid. Then do them! Sometimes we mask fear by calling it disinterest — bring it out in the open and go for it!

———————◆———————

Courage is the first of the human qualities because it is the quality which guarantees all the others. —*Winston Churchill*

———————◆———————

32

Learn The Art Of Influencing

I used to think "salesman" was a dirty word. (My apologies to all the great salespeople out there). If there was one thing I never wanted to be or be thought of, it was a salesperson. But I have drastically changed that view. I believe the ability to influence, persuade and sell ourselves and others is one of the most valuable skills a person can have. Nothing happens in this world without it.

Everyone needs to develop this skill. Whether it's a mother who needs to influence her children to do their best in school, a coach who wants to inspire his/her athletes, a CEO who needs to engage his/her employees in creating a successful company or an individual who wants to sell himself or herself to do something they have a fear about. I like to call it the *art* of influencing because I believe all great salespeople are artists.

In the dictionary, there are these definitions:
Art — *mastery; the application of skill or knowledge in*

a creative effort to produce works that have form or unusual perception; craftsmanship.

Influence — to awaken in another a purpose of disposition to act; to arouse one from lethargy or indifference to action; to have a positive effect on the behavior, development, action or thought of others; to prompt or stir.

Whether it's bad or good to sell depends on intention. If a person only wants to sell, persuade or influence for his/her own gain, that is a problem. But if one's intention is win/win and one cares about their "customers" — whether that's their children, employees, employer, clients or themselves — then having the skills to influence is a gift.

Give It A Go
Pick up a book on selling, go to a seminar, learn from someone you know who is great at persuading (with integrity). This week begin practicing the Art of Influencing. Here's a hint: it all begins with listening.

———————◆———————

Nothing is more validating and affirming than feeling understood. And the moment a person begins feeling understood, that person becomes far more open to influence and change. —*Stephen Covey*

———————◆———————

33

Celebrate

My sister-in-law took my nephew to gymnastics class when he was four or five years old. The teacher taught the children that every time they completed a somersault or any of the other exercises, they were supposed to stand tall with their arms outstretched out as if they had just landed the perfect vault in the Olympics.

One of the mothers came to class one day with a story. She had been in the kitchen and heard a noise and as she ran to see what it was, she saw her young son falling down the stairs (luckily carpeted). She watched in horror as he tumbled but when he got to the bottom, he stood up, threw his arms up in the air and flashed a big smile to *celebrate* his achievement.

I think we all tend to spend way too much time focusing on what isn't perfect, what we didn't do right, what we could have done better, and not nearly enough time congratulating ourselves and others. It has been proven time and again that positive reinforcement is the most effective and humanistic approach to training animals. Then why do we see people trying to change themselves, their children and their employees in the opposite manner? They try to create change by constantly bringing attention to mistakes and weaknesses.

It seems that very few of us take time to notice and *celebrate* small wins and then build on those. What would happen if every time you accomplished any small or large thing, you threw your arms in the air in celebration? I did it! I finished my paperwork! Yeah!

I used to have a team of salespeople and every time they had a great day, I would go in their area of the company and do my "celebration dance." It was silly but it came from my heart and made everyone laugh, even though they would shake their heads like I had lost my mind. Interestingly, after I left, someone told me that they had all felt sad because no one ever celebrated with them any more.

Take time to celebrate. Regularly give yourself and others a hearty pat on the back!

Give It A Go
There's no time like the present. Reach up with your right hand — right now — turn your palm around and pat yourself on the back! Now make sure that for the next week you celebrate at least twice a day — once for yourself and once for someone else's accomplishments. It doesn't matter how small the accomplishment is but make the celebration grander than you are accustomed to.

...make everyday a holiday and
celebrate just living! —*Amanda Bradley*

34

Be The Change You Want To See

When I was in my late 20s, I was complaining about my children to a friend. This friend, probably out of caring and maybe also a little frustration, took a chance. He cautiously said, "Debra, you keep talking about what *they* need to do, but what about *you?* I'm not sure that you are demonstrating to your kids the things that you want them to do. I hope I don't sound too harsh, but here's the bottom-line: *Your life is either going to be an example of how to be or, a warning of how not to be.* I think you need *to choose.*"

What audacity! I couldn't believe he had said that to me. But throughout the next week, the question kept running in my mind, "Am I being an example or a warning?" There were some areas where I felt like I was a pretty good example but unfortunately, I saw many more behaviors and attitudes that were warnings of how not to be. I was inspired. I made a commitment to someday be a person my children would look up to — a role model.

Since then, I've realized that there's even more to it. If there is any change we want to see in others, in our company, or even in the world, we need to demonstrate that change.

Try to look at yourself when you are bothered by someone else's behavior. Try hard to discover how you might be doing the same thing, maybe in a different context, but the same nevertheless. Start looking for how you can make the changes in yourself first. The fascinating thing is that when you do that, often you will begin to see the changes in others. Be patient.

Give It A Go
Are there any parts of your life where it's time for you to step up and be a better example? Also, test out the idea that anything you don't like in/about someone else is an opportunity for you to take a look at yourself. This isn't necessarily easy but try it anyway.

...and as we let our own light shine, we unconsciously give other people permission to do the same. As we are liberated from our own fear, our presence automatically liberates others.
—*Nelson Mandela*

35

Play The What If Game

The following situation is a dilemma that was presented to job applicants. How would you answer?

You are driving along on a wild stormy night. You pass by a bus stop, and you see three people waiting for the bus: 1. An elderly woman who is gravely ill, 2. An old friend who once saved your life, and 3. The perfect man (or) woman you have been dreaming about. Which one would you choose, knowing that there *could only be one passenger in your car*?

After your initial answer — try this. Ask yourself, "What if I could do something other than just choose one? What are my other options?"

The candidate who was hired (out of 200 applicants) answered like this, "I would give the car keys to my old friend, and let him take the lady to the hospital. Then I would stay behind and wait for the bus with the man of my dreams."

So often we put barriers up that don't need to exist. Just because limited options are presented (or thought of initially) doesn't mean that's all there is.

Make it a habit to ask yourself questions like: "What if there were no barriers? What else could I do? What options are there that I'm not thinking of? What else could this mean?   What other resources could be available? What if anything were possible? What if I could be, do, have, or create anything I wanted? What else could I try?

Give It A Go
Play the What If game at least once a day for a week. Stretch yourself and write down a minimum of 2-3 options in any given situation. Think of something that you didn't initially consider.   Assume that there is always one more possibility, then find it.

If I were to wish for anything, I should not wish for wealth and power, but for the passionate sense of the potential, for the eye which, ever young and ardent, sees the possible. Pleasure disappoints, possibility never. —*Soren Kierkegaard*

36

Use Your Creativity

I remember years ago saying to a good friend of mine, "I'm not creative. I'm just a boring stick-in-the-mud." It's almost inconceivable to me now that I used to believe that about myself. The biggest problem was that when I believed it, I wasn't tapping into the creativity we all possess. I was blocking an important resource — one that is available to each of us. Our creativity helps us overcome difficult situations, helps us to create success in any area of our lives and is part of the playful energy that allows us to really enjoy life.

Granted, some people have developed their creativity more than others but that doesn't mean we aren't all creative. I believe the first step in using your creativity to make your life more fun, interesting, successful, stimulating, and productive is to first acknowledge that *you are creative!*

When I started to tell myself I was creative, I became aware of how creative I really was. Noticing how I was *already* creative, encouraged me to explore and develop those abilities even more. I became more willing to experiment and make mistakes. This newfound creativity really paid off in my work by helping me find solutions to challenging business problems. It also helped me find ways to continuously make my life even more of an *E Ticket Ride.*

Julia Cameron, author of *The Artist's Way,* says that it's not a matter of *becoming* creative but about *letting* yourself be creative. If you want to develop and use your creativity more, it's a simple process of acknowledging it, letting go of fear and judgment, challenging yourself regularly and being willing to make mistakes.

Give It A Go
Choose a creativity affirmation. Then with enthusiasm, say it several times a day. Example — I use my innate creativity, daily, to create value for others and to find ways beyond any and all barriers to my goals.

———————•———————

A remarkable gift, creativity. No other aspect of the human psyche is as powerful. It can exist unused for many years and then, with the right encouragement, creativity can be expressed, improving our lives and the lives of everyone around us. —*C. Diane Ealy, PhD.*

———————•———————

37

Model Success

Whatever you want to be, do, have or create in your life, there is someone out there who is doing it, has done it or has done something similar. Why does this matter? Because that means if they can, so can you! Even if what you are learning from them is how to be the first at something.

Throughout history, it had been widely assumed that it was impossible for a human being to run a mile in under four minutes. Roger Bannister not only believed it was possible, but in 1954, he was the first person to break the four-minute mile when he ran it in 3:59:04. His record was only held for 46 days because when other people began to "model" Bannister's beliefs and training, they were also able to break the four-minute mile. Nevertheless, Roger Bannister's name was written into the record books and sporting folklore for being the first.

I find it interesting how often people do the opposite of modeling success. When they see someone who has accomplished something, they find fault, look for excuses of why that person has succeeded, or become resentful. What a waste! If there is something you want — find people who are successful in that area and learn, learn, learn from them.

When I first became a hairstylist, I was painfully shy and wouldn't talk to my customers. After a threat of losing my job if I didn't start to be more engaging, I *modeled* one of the stylists in my salon. I literally sat with a pad and pen and wrote down what he said to start and carry on conversations. Within a few weeks — I had begun to enjoy my customers more and luckily, I was able to keep my job.

Cut down on the learning curve — model success!

Give It A Go
Take a look at your goals and think of someone who has already accomplished something similar. Begin to model (learn from, copy, act as if, do what they do) until you begin producing a similar or better result.

———————•———————

Whatever your discipline, become a student of excellence in all things. Take every opportunity to observe people who manifest the qualities of mastery. These models of excellence will inspire you and guide you toward the fulfillment of your highest potential. *—Michael Gelb and Tony Buzan*

———————•———————

110

38

Invest In Yourself

The other day I was watching the *Today Show* and one of their featured financial advisors was talking about what to do with your income tax refund. One of the investments she recommended was that you invest in yourself. She suggested people use the money to further their education, learn a new skill, take a seminar...

I believe that investing in yourself is one of the most important and secure investments you can make. When all is said and done, there is no security in terms of financial investments, jobs, relationships, homes or cars. The only *real* security we have is knowing we can survive and *thrive* in any situation. I heard Will Smith in an interview once say, "I don't know how to swim, but I know I would never drown." He believes, he *knows* he can "make it" no matter what happens.

I attended conferences to improve my creative/ technical skills, my business skills and my communication skills when I was a hairstylist. Not only did my business continue to expand, but I grew as a person. By doing that, I was also better prepared when I moved into my next career.

Everything one learns can have multiple benefits. A person may be in school to learn more about computers but that will also build their confidence in their ability to learn in general. No one can go wrong by learning and growing.

Invest in yourself to build your internal confidence that you can learn, adapt, handle and succeed at anything. Invest in yourself to build the actual skills and knowledge you need to stay viable in your work, in your relationships and in your life. Invest in your health so that you are physically capable. What should you invest? Invest your time, invest your money and invest your energy!

Give It A Go
Congratulations! You are already investing in yourself by reading and applying the secrets in this book. Choose one specific area where you want or need to grow, learn and develop. This week make a definitive investment in that area.

———————•———————

I know of no more encouraging fact than the unquestionable ability of man to elevate his life by conscious endeavor. *—Henry David Thoreau*

———————•———————

39

Be Enthusiastic

The word enthusiasm came from the Greek word *enthousiazein* — to be inspired. Enthusiasm helps us get past adversity, allows us to spread positive energy, encourages and inspires others and is generally priceless! Enthusiasm is a necessary ingredient in living an *E Ticket Life.*

Sometimes enthusiasm has a negative association. People may think of *rah—rah* cheerleaders from high school or game show contestants, but the truth is that enthusiasm and passion are the fuel behind every great achievement. Think of the opposite — apathy, indifference and lethargy. Those things literally suck the life energy out of you and will never get you the life you want.

So how do you create enthusiasm? Dr. Norman Vincent Peale suggests this: *"Think excitement, talk excitement, act out excitement and you are bound to become an excited person. Life will take on a new zest, deeper interest and greater meaning. You can think, talk and act yourself into dullness or into monotony or unhappiness. By the same process you can build up inspiration, excitement and surging depths of joy."*

Sometimes I'll walk around a company before I conduct a program with them. It's fascinating to see people with scowls on their faces who don't speak or greet anyone. These are the same people complaining about how they don't enjoy their job. I often tell people, if you aren't happy in this job, be careful because guess who's is going with you to the next one.

With one client, I conducted my program, The Breakthrough Experience™, four days a week for thirteen weeks. Sometimes, I would wake up exhausted and feeling like I couldn't do one more day. I knew that in order to give my best, I needed my full energy and enthusiasm. I had it in my heart, but I needed to also have it in my body. I would walk around my apartment before I left, dancing and "acting as if" I was excited about going. After only a few minutes, my energy would increase and I was able to show up and share my enthusiasm with that special group of people.

Act enthusiastic and you'll find yourself feeling more enthusiastic.

Give It A Go
For one entire week approach your day with enthusiasm. Try enthusiastically cleaning your room, working on a report, dealing with a difficult person. You'll be amazed at how much better you feel and the great results you'll get.

You can do anything if you have enthusiasm.
Enthusiasm is the yeast that makes your hopes
rise to the stars. Enthusiasm is the spark in
your eye, the swing in your gait, the grip of
your hand, the irresistible surge of your will
and your energy to execute your ideas.
Enthusiasts are fighters, they have fortitude,
they have staying qualities. Enthusiasm is at
the bottom of all progress! With it, there is
accomplishment. Without it there are
only alibis. —Henry Ford

40

Eliminate Time And Money Excuses

If you don't want to do something — admit it outright. If you are afraid — say that. If you aren't sure how — that's fine, but stop using the infamous, *I can't because I don't have the time or I can't because I don't have the money.*

The biggest problem with using these time and money excuses is that if we say them often enough, we begin to believe that they're true — *then they become true and we are trapped.* I know that limited time and/or money can be major barriers for some people but they are barriers that can be overcome. You can go around, over, through or under these limitations— there is always a way if you want something badly enough.

If money were the *real* reason, then no one who had been poor would ever have made a success of themselves. If limited time were the *real* reason, then no single mother would have managed to raise her kids, work *and* go to school. Again, I'm not saying that these things are not barriers, but they don't have to stop you from making your life the way you really want it to be.

Since these used to be excuses I used on a regular basis, I know what it takes to get past them. The first thing it takes is to stop saying you don't have the time or money! Be honest. Say, "I don't want that badly enough to find the time for it.", "It's not important enough for me to put the energy into to figuring out a way to purchase it", or "I *will* find a way!" By doing that, you will start sending the message to your brain that *it is your choice*. Then you are free to engage your creativity in finding ways around those barriers.

For centuries, when people have wanted something badly enough, they have found their way past the barriers of time and money. You can too!

Give It A Go
Begin now to catch yourself every time you say anything similar to, "I can't afford that," or "I'm too busy." Immediately change it to something that puts you in control. Whether that's, "I choose not to or I will find a way!"

He that is good at making excuses is seldom good at anything else. —*Benjamin Franklin*

41

Be Flexible

I believe that flexibility in our bodies, in our minds and in our hearts makes us strong. When a person's body is rigid and unbending they have fewer choices of how they can use their body. When a person restricts their thinking, they are in trouble when presented with this world of hyper-change. When a person's heart hardens, they miss opportunities for love, compassion and joy. Flexibility, on the other hand, creates choice.

Everyone knows that creating a more flexible body requires stretching. But even if a person has developed excellent flexibility in their body, without continued stretching, it will slowly begin to seize up and become rigid. Obviously, it is the same with a person's thinking.

Is there anything you should not be flexible on? Certainly, but choose carefully. Determine what your core values and principles are and hold steady to those. In the United States, there is a core value or principle upon which the country was based which states: "...that all men are created equal, that they are endowed by their Creator with certain unalienable Rights, that among these are Life, Liberty, and the pursuit of Happiness." That foundational value remains steady while ways to realize it continue to evolve.

I have learned to stay focused on my goals but to be extremely flexible in finding better, faster, more effortless ways to get there. More importantly, I've learned to pay more attention to what's really important and soften my heart and my approach to everything else.

Another hint: Stay unwavering on your goals but be very flexible in how you get there.

Give It A Go
Notice when you tend to get resistant or stuck. Practice flexibility. Be willing to change your approach, your thinking and your emotional reactions. Flexibility is power!

———————•———————

I can't change the direction of the wind.
But I can adjust my sails. —Anon

———————•———————

42

Be A Straight Shooter

Being a straight shooter means that you are honest — first with yourself and then with others. It means you don't hold your feelings and thoughts back out of fear. I can't tell you how many meetings I've been in over the years where a group sat around a table talking about the problems (as they saw them) and as soon as the boss entered the room, everyone did their best impression of a clam. I don't get it! Ok, I know it's a little scary sometimes to say what you think, but are the alternatives really better options?

Some of the alternatives are — covering up your true feelings, letting your fear of how someone is going to view you keep you quiet; saying one thing when you really mean something else; trying to hide problems or outright lying. Trying to build any relationship, family structure or business based on lies and half-truths is like trying to build a skyscraper on a cracking, unstable foundation. It can look good on the surface but it will crumble. The real question is — are you willing to trade the potential of short-term discomfort for the long-term benefits?

Begin with being honest and straight-forward with yourself. Don't sidestep your true feelings or avoid looking at your behaviors. It will only catch up with you later. From a place of honesty with yourself, you can build strong, healthy, safe relationships in business, with friends, and family based on that same principle of honest communication.

Sometimes the truth hurts. So I'll wrap this up with *my* ongoing lesson. Learn to combine the truth with love, kindness, humor and compassion. There is almost always a way to say what you need to say with more awareness. The better you become at being a "straight shooter" gracefully and tactfully, the better it will be received and the more at ease you will feel.

Give It A Go
Notice where you are holding back or not being truthful with yourself or others. Take a chance. You know the places in your life where you need to be more of a straight-shooter — there's no time like the present.

———•———

You must speak straight so that your
words may go as sunlight to our hearts.
—*Cochise, Cherokee Warrior*

———•———

43

Be Optimistic

Have you ever noticed that pessimists are often thought of as more realistic, while optimists can be looked at as unrealistic? And yet, clinical research proves that optimists are more successful in school, in marriages, in their work (and there is even evidence that indicates that they live longer). Pessimists tend to give up more easily and traditionally experience more depression.

Of course, there are a lot of people who *think* they are optimistic when, in reality, they speak and act like a pessimist. On occasion, I have found myself falling into this category.

At one point in my career I decided I wanted to develop business in Europe. On my first trip over there to begin this process, I noticed that I was being *realistic* in my thinking. I was saying things to myself like, "Don't count on this working. If it doesn't work out, that's ok." I thought I was being *realistic* but I finally realized — I was just trying to protect myself from disappointment.

Even though I see myself as an optimist, I've noticed there have been other times in my life that I've found myself falling into *realistic* or even pessimistic traps. Usually this has been when I've tried something many times and have not yet gotten the results I'm going for. For me, that's when it gets harder to be optimistic but...

The most important time to be optimistic is when things are difficult. Optimism is a fuel that helps you keep going through those difficult times, allows you to creatively approach barriers and is an intelligent *choice*.

Give It A Go

This week pay close attention to where and when you tend toward optimism or pessimism. If you catch yourself being pessimistic — make the choice to immediately turn it around. Try taking the optimism test in a very interesting book called, *Learned Optimism*, by Martin E.P. Seligman, PhD.

―――――――――――――•―――――――――――――

No pessimist ever discovered the secrets of the stars, or sailed to an uncharted land, or opened a new heaven to the human spirit. *―Helen Keller*

―――――――――――――•―――――――――――――

44

Promote Positive Flow

There is a flow in the universe. That can be a flow of energy, love, money, kindness, generosity... or it can also be a flow of fear, anger, depression, lack... It's up to you to promote and benefit from the positive flow.

The first rule of being in positive flow is to give what you want to receive. If you want more love, be more loving. If you want more money, be more generous. If you want people to listen to you more, be a more active listener. If you want more happiness, give a happier you to others. And on and on... Many of us hold back out of fear but all we are doing is keeping ourselves from the very thing we want.

The second rule of being in positive flow is to become comfortable with receiving, as well as, giving. A friend helped me learn this lesson. I needed a printer and one of the participants in a seminar I was teaching wanted to give me a brand new one (he worked for a big computer company). I politely rejected his offer because I hadn't *earned* the printer. I blocked the flow. After reading a wonderful book called, *The Trick To Money Is Having Some* by Stuart Wilde, I learned about flow and, as it related to money, I saw how I was constantly blocking it in my life.

I decided to call this person back and accept his generous offer. When I did, I found out that I had not only prevented myself from receiving something I needed, but he felt very hurt. He was concerned that I thought he wanted something from me. He had spent two weeks trying to figure out how to get me the printer without my knowing it came from him. That lesson helped me begin to increase the flow of money and financial success into my life.

Get the flow going. Where do you need to stimulate a more positive flow in your life?

Give It A Go
Think of something you want in your life but don't feel you are getting enough of. This week, consciously give that very thing — then make sure when it comes back to you, graciously accept. You may find, though that it comes back from somewhere other than where you gave it.

———————————•———————————

Life begets life. Energy creates energy. It is by spending oneself that one becomes rich.
—*Sarah Bernhardt*

———————————•———————————

45

Take Chances

I have a news flash! Safety is an illusion. So many people are running around trying to protect every-thing. They are trying to protect their money, protect their reputations, protect their hearts... I suppose it makes sense, sometimes, to cover your bases and/or have a back-up plan. That said, no one I know who has been exceptionally successful is very cautious or tentative.

Fear can be a wonderful emotion — it can save our lives — but, if not managed, it can clip our wings and keep us from living fully. People who are older or who have more experience will tell you that if they had it to do over again, they would have risked more and feared less. Besides — everything is a risk and what people are afraid of is often inconsequential compared to the potential payoff. Let your inner voice be your guide.

Walking out of your house is a risk; staying in your house is a risk. Loving is a risk; not loving is a risk.

Trying to always be "safe" from life is probably the biggest risk of all! The more we try to protect ourselves from loss, hurt, failure, embarrassment... the thicker the barriers become to love, success, wealth, happiness, fun and living life fully.

Successful people know that even if one appears to "fail," there is an opportunity to learn something that can help next time. We encourage children to take chances. We tell them to speak up in class, try soccer, ask that special person on a date... We need to take our own advice.

Don't get so "old" that you stop growing, risking, trying and taking chances! Be happy about that little nervousness you feel when you step out there. It means you are still alive and growing. Take some chances, make some mistakes. That is part of the formula for success.

Give It A Go
This week take a chance at least once each day. Get in the habit of taking small risks so that you build the needed muscle for the bigger ones!

We cannot escape fear. We can only transform
it into a companion that accompanies us on
all our exciting adventures. Take a risk a day —
one small or bold stroke that will make you feel
great once you have done it. —*Susan Jeffers*

46

See The Best In People

There are over six billion people in the world. I believe that a big secret to living a successful life is learning to like, enjoy and work together with the people with whom we share the planet (or for that matter — our offices). How can we do this when we come from such different races, cultures, religions, educations and values? One simple way is to consistently look for the best in people. Look for the good, the interesting, the entertaining, the possibilities... Granted, you may have to look harder with some people but I promise you that most of the time you will find what you are looking for.

The first time I traveled to New York City was in the late 70s and I was so excited to see "real" New Yorkers. Having grown up in Mississippi, I was taught that those "Yankees" were rude, loud, uncaring swindlers and that I had better watch my back. Fortunately, instead of hearing rude, loud, uncaring, swindlers — I heard straight-forward, intense, unique and immensely interesting.

And that's precisely what I found in New York — wonderful, straight-forward, intense, unique and immensely interesting people! Big surprise? Definitely not! Because we all tend to see precisely what we are looking for, we are rarely disappointed. I've had someone say to me, "Well, that's very 'Pollyanna' of you but there is a real world out there and some people are very bad. If you don't have your defenses up, you can get hurt."

It's true that some people may hurt us, so my caveat is this: See The Best In People and *remain aware*. Be smart and trust your instincts. But don't let a small minority keep you from liking people and being someone who draws out the good in others. The more you see the best in people, the more they will give you their best. Many of your greatest times will come from your experiences with others, but it starts with you.

Give It A Go
Find someone that you don't particularly like and decide to look at them differently. Look for things you can appreciate, respect, find funny or interesting about them. Make it a game to genuinely find something you can like in everyone you know or meet. The icing on the cake is to **tell them.**

———————◆———————

If you want to get the best out of a man, you must look for the best that is in him. —*Bernard Haldane*

———————◆———————

47

Stay Present

Have you ever been working but you were really thinking about something you needed to do at home? Have you been with a client when you were thinking about something your boss had said to you earlier that morning? Have you ever been with the man or woman you love and you were worrying about work? Most of us have done this too many times in our lives.

You've probably also had the wonderful experience of being with your spouse, your boss, your doctor, a friend or your child when you could *sense* that they were fully present to you. How did that feel? It is usually an amazing experience for both parties. Your life is a series of moments added up together. One way to create a life you love is to engage yourself fully in the present and make the most of those moments.

The daughter of a dear man I know is suffering from multiple sclerosis. He is spending his time seeing her through the last days (maybe months) of her life. He is a true model to me of a person staying present. Here is an excerpt from an email I received from him about one of his mornings with Yarra.

"I told her that for years I was the teacher and she was the pupil and that now the roles had been reversed. I was learning from her to graciously and lovingly let go of my body as I liberated my Spirit. To be more accepting of my gifts and challenges, to be present in the moment, to be at peace with who I am and where I am. The time was magical; it was really timeless and spaceless. Even though she is unable to speak, we have great interactions. At one point I even playfully said, 'Tell me another joke.' She said nothing then I laughed, and said, 'I really liked that one but you've told it before.' We laughed and laughed together. If this was all that there was of my lifetime, it would have been enough, thank you GOD."

Give It A Go
This week stay present to whomever you are with, whatever you are doing. Consciously decide to practice two things: 1) Be in the moment; 2) Enjoy the moment. Do this as many times throughout each day as you possibly can. Write your experiences in your journal.

May the light of life illuminate my world and in the center may there always be a soft, quiet space where soul and spirit connect to blend time and space, matter and myth, laughter and tears and may I visit often with wisdom from yesterday and hope for tomorrow while accepting today as the only one in which I can be fully present. —*Chris Amoroso (father from the previous story)*

48

Be Grateful

When I first started on my quest to create an *E Ticket Life*, I thought that creating a life I loved was all about changing everything. I've since realized that in order to create anything, a person needs to begin with something. Taking stock of your current gifts gives you something with which to build and create. It helps you be present to and *realize how fortunate and wealthy you already are.* From that understanding it is easier to choose where you want to go next.

W. Mitchell is a man who has personally inspired me. When I met him many years ago, I first saw a terribly disfigured man in a wheelchair. But when I approached him and we talked, I saw a vibrant, happy person who is living a fulfilling and successful life.

Mitchell was a very successful business owner when he crashed his motorcycle and suffered burns over 65% of his body. About four years later, after he was back on his feet and making millions as the head of a new company, he was set back again. Ice on the wings of the plane he was flying forced him to make an emergency landing and paralyzed him from the waist down. He had gone through physical and mental agony but *Mitchell chose to be grateful* for and focus on what he still had and what he could still do. He likes to say, "Before all of this happened to me, there were 10,000 things I could do, now, there are 9,000. Sure, I could dwell on the 1,000 that I can't do. But I prefer to think about the 9,000 that are left." Mitchell went on to become mayor of Crested Butte, Colorado, and is the author of *It's Not What Happens to You, It's What You Do About It.*

Give It A Go
Take a few minutes each day this week and think about (better yet, write down) at least ten things you are grateful for. Each day write down ten new ones so that by the end of the week you will have at least seventy things to be grateful for. You can include small things from your current day. Being grateful is a positive habit — what if you did this for a year?

Gratitude unlocks the fullness of life. It turns what we have into enough and more. It turns denial into acceptance, chaos to order, confusion to clarity. It can turn a meal into a feast, a house into a home, a stranger into a friend. Gratitude makes sense of our past, brings peace for today and creates a vision for tomorrow.
—*Melody Beattie*

49

Treat Your Body Right

If you're not alive, it's a little challenging to create the life you want. Cardiovascular disease, principally heart disease and stroke, is a leading killer of both men and women among all racial and ethnic groups. Warding off this disease (and many others) is within your control. So take charge and treat your body right because being healthy will give you more longevity and allow you more choices.

There are many people in the world who are dealing with severe physical problems and diseases that are not directly related to their lifestyles. In spite of that, they have found ways to create purposeful and ful-filling lives (I think of Christopher Reeves) so, health and happiness don't have to be directly linked. With that said, to the degree we have control over it, tak-ing great care of the vessel we live in makes a lot of sense. Make friends with your body, love it and care for it. It's the only one you get this time around.

Although there are countless programs for healthy living, there are some basics that are common to them all.

- Exercise your body regularly
- Eat good food
- Drink lots of water
- Get enough rest
- Breathe deeply
- Get the vitamins you need
- Don't smoke

Also, there are many ways in this book for managing your emotional health which will also help you take care of your body. When we are happy and feeling good it has a tremendously positive impact on our health – it's all related!

Give It A Go

Take stock of the good things you are currently doing to care for your health. Then be honest with what you still need to do to treat your body right. Begin now.

Health is so necessary to all the duties, as well as pleasures of life, that the crime of squandering it is equal to the folly.

—Samuel Johnson

50

Dream Bigger

Years ago, I didn't know how to dream big. It never occurred to me to wish for anything that seemed to be outside my perceived possibilities. Dreaming big to me meant hoping that someday we could have that apartment that cost $100 a month instead of the one we were living in that was $75 a month. I couldn't see any point in dreaming of traveling the world, making lots of money, or being free to explore and learn. I hadn't yet developed my Dream Bigger muscle.

The bottom line is that it is extremely rare that anything wonderful comes to us unless we first have the seed or thought. We must employ our imagination in opening the door to new possibilities for ourselves. Most of us have heard the quote from Napoleon Hill, "What the mind of man can conceive and believe, the mind of man can achieve." But few people make the connection that *if we don't dream it, it's unlikely we will ever achieve it.*

You can start by dreaming a little bigger. Begin to stretch your imagination as to what is possible. When you think of something you want to be, do, have or create — let your mind wander beyond what you are currently thinking. Then stretch a little farther. Let go of any fear about failures or mistakes. It's like Les Brown says, "Shoot for the moon. Even if you miss it you will land among the stars."

Be prepared, though. Big dreamers are some-times discouraged or even ridiculed by small dreamers. Often, small dreamers are just trying to protect their friends and/or family from possible disappointment or maybe they are trying to defend their own small thinking. It really doesn't matter why.

Just remember, nothing big was ever accomplished through small thinking.

Give It A Go
Go back to the exercise from the first section — Begin With The End In Mind — and experiment with dreaming bigger. What if *anything* were possible? Let your imagination go!

———————————•———————————

We aim above the mark to hit the mark.
—Ralph Waldo Emerson

———————————•———————————

51

Love What You Do

How do you create the career of your dreams? There are two ways. First, and probably most appealing is this: *Turn what you love to do (and that you are good at) into your career.* Here is a great model for looking at this: Think of a bull's eye with four rings. In the outside ring (Ring 4) are the things you are no good at doing. In the next ring (Ring 3) are the things that you are adequate at or capable of doing. In the ring closest to the center (Ring 2) are the things that you excel at. Most people spend the majority of their time in Rings 2 and 3. They do jobs in which they are capable, maybe even excellent but which don't give them the "juice".

The center ring (Ring 1) is the target. In this ring are the things you excel at doing which you also love. The most successful people, the ones most fulfilled in their careers and often those earning the most money spend the majority of their time in the center ring. What do you love to do? Make sure you grow your skills to match and you will have the career you *really* want.

The second is this: If you are in the process of building your skills in the thing you love but you still need to earn a living during that time, then *find ways within your current job to learn, grow and enjoy what you do.* I'm sure you have already found many ideas in this book that will help you improve your satisfaction, your skills and possibly even your income, without even changing jobs. There are some old song lyrics that say, "If you can't be with the one you love, then love the one you're with."

Learning to make the most of your current situation will only help you as you grow into the career you *really* want!

Give It A Go
Begin a list of everything you enjoy doing. Brainstorm ways of how you might earn money doing those things. Continue the list and the brainstorm until something clicks for you. Also, pick up a great career finding book called, *What Color Is Your Parachute?* by Richard Nelson Bolles

---

Find out what you like doing best and get someone to pay you for doing it." —*Katharine Whitehorn*

52

Everything Is Perfect

In the year 2000 I began noticing that for the first time in many years I was feeling sad — teetering on depressed. I couldn't quite identify the reason but the feeling was tugging at the edges of my consciousness. One day while sitting at my kitchen table thinking about my life, I realized what my problem was. Unwittingly, I had created a scenario all those years ago when I came up with my wonderful idea of living an *E Ticket Life* where I envisioned my life with a partner, and I was still single.

You may remember reading in the introduction that when I first did *The Rocking Chair Test* I was unhappily married and looking for fulfillment. At that time, I made my decision to get a divorce, partly based on the idea that finding the relationship of my dreams would be an *E Ticket Ride*. What I didn't realize was that, unconsciously, I had set up another belief. If I *didn't* find that perfect relationship, then my life would not be an *E Ticket Ride*. So there I was at age forty-seven and I hadn't found the relationship of my dreams. That's why I was feeling sad and a little depressed.

Then I had what can only be called a spiritual experience. A beam of light shown directly on me from the skylight and I was filled with the following knowledge — *everything is perfect* (at this moment and always). I felt a peace I had never experienced before and I sat there for hours reveling in my new understanding. I have continued to revel in this understanding ever since.

During my first thirty-three years, I often wondered, "why me?" I felt like a victim and my life reflected that thinking.

The next fourteen years led me to believe something that helped me immensely. I accepted that everything had a reason and a purpose and would serve me if I let it. This way of thinking gave me confidence and the ability to deal with challenges.

The problem during those fourteen years was that I would still feel annoyed, and sometimes angry, when things weren't going my way. Even though I believed that there was an opportunity for these situations to serve me somewhere down the line, I wasn't able to feel the perfection of the situation in that moment.

My new understanding, gained under the skylight in my kitchen, is a small nuance on my previous philosophy that everything has a reason and a purpose and will someday serve me. The nuance is this: *This moment is perfect. I don't have to wait for someday.*

146

This slight change in perception has had an immeasurable impact in my life. Knowing that everything is perfect in this moment (not someday) allows me to truly embrace whatever happens. When something occurs that I don't like, I take a deep breath and know that *all is as it should be right now and always.*

From that calm and centered place, I'm much better at choosing the best course of action. I've found that by not resisting (which results in my annoyance or anger), I'm better able to sense the best way to respond to people and situations. This makes me much more effective, and much happier, both personally and professionally.

I lead a workshop called The Breakthrough Experience™. It's a very high-energy program that teaches people how to transcend barriers. The workshop culminates in all the participants (if they choose to) breaking a 1" thick, wood board — karate style. I have taught this program many times for entire organizations and attendance is often mandatory.

Sometimes, one or more participants will enter the room in a skeptical or resistant frame of mind. Previously, if every single person in the audience didn't love the workshop immediately, I felt that I wasn't doing a good job. I would focus on trying to change their *seemingly* negative attitude. This focus put a lot of pressure on me (and them) and I would feel drained at the end of a program.

Shortly after my realization that everything is perfect, I had a project with a hospital in New York. I conducted forty workshops of The Breakthrough Experience™ — two per day, four days a week for five weeks. These forty workshops were effortless and fun. When someone didn't respond the way I'd hoped, I just reminded myself that everything was perfect, smiled and continued teaching. Inevitably, a moment would present itself and I would sense just the right thing to say or do that would have the most impact with that person. More people came up to talk with me afterwards than ever before. The response to my programs, which had always been excellent, went through the roof!

Accepting that everything is as it should be has had a profound and positive impact in my life. I can't really call my acceptance of perfection a "strategy" because there is little to do when you understand and know that everything is perfect in the now. You may want to breathe deeply when you feel annoyance or anger and release your resistance. Acceptance of life's perfection is a state of being that I offer to you for consideration.

It's up to you.

We have come to the end of this part of our journey together. I *almost* missed the life I'm so fortunate to live now. Your heart of hearts knows the life that is waiting for you. I trust that you found something within these pages that will be helpful in your journey to realizing the life you *really* want.

I hope you will visit this book many times over the years and share it with friends and family. I'd love to hear from you or someday maybe we'll have the opportunity to meet in person. Until then...

I send you love, deep wishes that your all dreams come true, and a reminder to always...

Enjoy The Ride!

—Debra Russell

...start thinking of yourself as an artist and your life as a work-in-progress. Works-in-progress are never perfect. But changes can be made...Art evolves. So does life. Art is never stagnant. Neither is life. The beautiful, authentic life you are creating for yourself is your art. It's the highest art.
—Sarah Ban Breathnach